101 WINNING WAYS

101 Winning Attitudes for Swimming and Life!

by Nick Baker – Peak Performance Swim Camp

No portion of this book may be reproduced or used in any form or by any means, electronic or mechanical, including photocopying, recording, or by any information storage and retrieval system, without prior written permission of the author.

DEDICATION

This book is dedicated to swimmers of all ages and abilities who commit countless hours in pursuit of their swimming dreams.

INTRODUCTION

Swimming is a very competitive sport. To be competitive, you need the right winning attitudes or 'winning ways.' Winning attitudes act like automatic pilots, guiding you to victory.

The pages in this book identify 101 winning attitudes, attitudes all great swimmers possess – including Michael Phelps. **101 Winning Ways** presents these winning attitudes in an easy-to-read, easy-to-understand format. The creative cartoons and simple text make learning fun and easy.

While physical fitness and technical know-how are keys to swimming success - nothing, absolutely nothing, can replace the winning attitudes found in this book.

WINNERS WIN BECAUSE THEY BEGIN

They can't wait...
to start winning.

1

WINNERS TAKE IT IN STRIDE

They take the bad...with the good.

WINNERS KEEP THEIR COOL

They keep themselves under control...and that keeps them in control.

WINNERS LIVE IN THE PRESENT...NOT THE PAST

They know it's what they do today, not what they did yesterday...that will lead to a brighter tommorrow.

WINNERS PLAY THE HAND THEY'RE DEALT

They do the very best...
with what they have.

5

WINNERS BUILD ON THEIR STRENGTHS

They use their strengths...to make them stronger.

WINNERS GIVE IT THEIR ALL...NOT THEIR ALMOST

They know if they want to move forward...they can't afford to hold anything back.

7

WINNERS USE IT...THEY DON'T ABUSE IT

They don't let their talents...
go to waste

WINNERS STEP OUTSIDE THEIR COMFORT ZONE

They know staying comfortable ...means staying put.

9

WINNERS GET DOWN TO BUSINESS

They get to work...when there's work to be done.

WINNERS CIRCULATE... THEY DON'T HIBERNATE

They don't wait for things to happen ...they make things happen.

WINNERS PAY THEIR DUES

They willingly do what they must do...
to become what they want to become.

WINNERS ARE OPEN TO SUGGESTIONS

They'll make a change
...if it's a change
for the better.

WINNERS DELIVER THE GOODS

They can be counted on...when it counts.

WINNERS PULL THEIR OWN WEIGHT

They do their fair
share...of the work.

WINNERS PLAY FAIR

They know the only way to really win...
is to play by the rules.

WINNERS ARE FLEXIBLE

They find by giving a little...
they get a lot in return.

WINNERS BEAT THE COMPETITION TO THE PUNCH

They get ahead...by getting a head
start on the competition.

WINNERS NEVER GO IT ALONE

They know they need the
help of others...to
help themselves.

19

WINNERS AREN'T SET IN THEIR WAYS

They don't let the way they are...
stand in the way of becoming
someone better.

WINNERS ARE ALL EARS

They're eager
to listen...
ready to learn.

21

WINNERS KNOW WHEN TO HOLD ON...AND WHEN TO LET GO

They know when it's time to keep trying... and when it's time to try something new.

WINNERS GO WITH THE FLOW

They adjust...to any situation.

23

WINNERS ARE ENERGY EFFICIENT

They don't waste their energy...on things that are a waste of time.

WINNERS ARE HOOKED ON

uccess

They have a need
...to succeed.

WINNERS KNOW ACTIONS SPEAK LOUDER THAN WORDS

They don't just talk about it...
they do something about it.

WINNERS ARE GAME FOR ALMOST ANYTHING

They're willing to give it a try...
even though they've never
tried it before.

WINNERS HAVE THE COURAGE OF THEIR CONVICTIONS

They stand up...for what they believe in.

WINNERS GRAB THE BULL BY THE HORNS

They fearlessly face...any challenge facing them.

29

WINNERS KNOW THERE'S NO SHAME IN FAILING...ONLY IN FAILING TO DO THEIR BEST

They know that all they can do is the best they can do...and that's good enough for them.

WINNERS KNOW THEY MUST SOMETIMES LOSE TO WIN

They know to get better...
they need to go up against
better competition.

31

WINNERS DO WITHIN...WHILE THEY DO WITHOUT

They keep working hard...even when things aren't working out.

WINNERS CAN TAKE A PUNCH

They won't let defeat
...knock them off
their feet.

WINNERS DREAM BIG...
BUT TAKE SMALL STEPS

They achieve their goals...one
step at a time.

WINNERS KEEP THEIR GOALS IN SIGHT AND SHINING BRIGHT

They never lose sight...
of what they're striving for.

WINNERS DON'T GET BENT OUT OF SHAPE

They don't let the pressures of trying
to be the best...get the better of them.

WINNERS PAT THEMSELVES ON THE BACK FOR A JOB WELL DONE

They give themselves credit...when credit is due.

WINNERS HAVE A LOT TO LEARN

They know...they don't know it all.

WINNERS ARE MORE LIKE ELEPHANTS AND LESS LIKE ALLIGATORS

They have big ears and small mouths... not big mouths and small ears.

39

WINNERS FOCUS MORE ON THE PLEASURES AND LESS ON THE PRESSURES OF WINNING

They remember...to keep it fun.

WINNERS OPEN THE DOOR WHEN OPPORTUNITY KNOCKS

They take advantage of every opportunity... that comes their way.

WINNERS KNOW THEY'RE GOOD AND THAT'S GOOD ENOUGH FOR THEM

They don't let what others think about them...change the way they think about themselves.

WINNERS SEE THEMSELVES AS WINNERS

They believe who they see...is who they'll become.

43

WINNERS GO ABOVE AND BEYOND THE CALL OF DUTY

They do more than is required...not less.

WINNERS ADD PERSPIRATION TO THEIR INSPIRATION

They don't just dream about it... they do something about it.

45

WINNERS PAY THE PRICE...
THEY SACRIFICE

They're willing to give up one thing...
to have another.

47

WINNERS HAVE PRIDE ON THEIR SIDE

They let their pride shine through...
in everything they do.

WINNERS WALK WITH THEIR HEADS HELD HIGH

They're proud...
of who they are.

49

WINNERS PACE THEMSELVES

They know when to push hard...and
when to pull back.

WINNERS KEEP THEIR HEADS ABOVE WATER

They somehow manage to handle... everything that comes their way.

WINNERS LAY IT ON THE LINE

They're willing to risk it all...to have it all.

WINNERS LEAD...

...THEY DON'T FOLLOW

They know if they follow the rest... they'll end up second best.

WINNERS KNOW THAT THINGS WON'T CHANGE... UNLESS THEY DO

They know if they change what's on the inside...the outside will take care of itself.

WINNERS CONTAIN NO ARTIFICIAL INGREDIENTS

They don't pretend to be...something they're not.

WINNERS SPEAK
NO EVIL

They say it in a positive way...
or they say nothing at all.

They stay positive...by not listening to negative talk.

WINNERS GIVE 101%

They give it all they've got...and
more if they have to.

WINNERS DON'T GO HALFWAY
...THEY GO ALL THE WAY

They finish...
what they start.

59

WINNERS LEAD A WELL BALANCED LIFE

They live their best...to be the best.

WINNERS HANG OUT WITH WINNERS

They like to be with people...like themselves.

61

WINNERS NEVER QUIT

They won't quit...no matter
how bad it gets.

WINNERS FACE UP TO THE PROBLEM FACING THEM

They know the best way to get rid of a problem...is to deal with it.

WINNERS ARE IN IT...TO WIN IT

They don't play at winning...they work at it.

WINNERS ASK FOR HELP WHEN THINGS PILE UP

They're not too shy or too proud...to ask for help when they need it.

65

WINNERS NEVER TAKE SUCCESS FOR GRANTED

They stay ahead...by not letting success go to their head.

WINNERS BLAZE NEW TRAILS

They willingly go...
where no one has
gone before.

WINNERS BITE THE BULLET

They willingly do...what they don't want to do.

WINNERS FACE THE MUSIC

They don't hide from the truth...they face up to it.

WINNERS NEVER MAKE THE SAME MISTAKE TWICE

They learn...from their mistakes.

WINNERS HAVE A HABIT OF BREAKING BAD HABITS

They stop doing the things... that might stop them from succeeding.

WINNERS KNOW PLAYING IT TOO SAFE CAN BE DANGEROUS

They know they must take chances...
to make advances.

WINNERS FEEL THE FEAR AND DO IT ANYWAY

They won't let fear...stand in the way of success.

WINNERS DON'T STEW... THEY DO

They know staying upset...
means staying put.

WINNERS BOUNCE

They don't let setbacks...set them back.

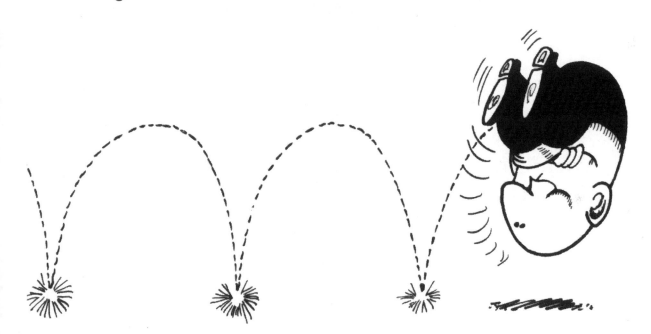

WINNERS NEVER SAY NEVER

They know it's never a question of if...
only a question of when.

WINNERS LEAVE NO STONE UNTURNED

They keep looking...
until they find
the solution.

77

WINNERS HAVE A THIRST TO BE FIRST

They won't stop...until they reach the top.

WINNERS SEE SUCCESS IN 3-D

SUCCESS

DESIRE

DEDICATION

DETERMINATION

They see desire, dedication and determination ...as keys to success.

WINNERS KEEP THE FAITH

They believe in themselves...
when others don't.

WINNERS LOOK FOR THE LIGHT AT THE END OF THE TUNNEL

They look for reasons
to keep going...when
things aren't going their way.

WINNERS COUNT THEIR BLESSINGS

They're grateful...for what they have.

WINNERS SEE THE GLASS HALF FULL...NOT HALF EMPTY

They see what they have...not what they have not.

WINNERS FORGIVE AND FORGET

They forgive themselves when they make a mistake...then forget about it.

WINNERS CELEBRATE THEIR SUCCESS

They take time out to feel good...about doing good.

WINNERS DON'T DELAY...
THEY DO IT TODAY

They don't put off until tomorrow...
what they could be doing today.

WINNERS DON'T COUNT THE DAYS... THEY MAKE THE DAYS COUNT

They see each day
...as another day
to get better.

87

WINNERS PLAN FOR THE FUTURE

They know where they're going... and how they're going to get there.

WINNERS SHOOT FOR THE MOON

They set goals that seem...far beyond their reach.

89

WINNERS KNOW THAT A POSITIVE LESSON ISN'T ALWAYS TAUGHT IN A POSITIVE WAY

They know something good...can come out of a bad experience.

WINNERS DON'T CRY OVER SPILT MILK

They know they
can't undo...
what's
already
been done.

WINNERS STRAIN TO GAIN

They give their utmost...to get
the very most.

WINNERS SWEAT THE SMALL STUFF

They know paying attention to the little things...will make a big difference.

WINNERS BELIEVE THERE'S A SOLUTION TO EVERY PROBLEM

They believe that things...have
a way of working out.

WINNERS KNOW THAT SUCCESS COMES IN CANS - NOT CANNOTS

They can –
because they
think they can.

WINNERS GO WITH THEIR HUNCHES

They trust...their intuition.

WINNERS DON'T JUMP TO CONCLUSIONS

They check it out...when in doubt.

WINNERS HAVE A PASSION FOR EXCELLENCE

They thrive...on being the best.

WINNERS KNOW NOTHING SUCCEEDS LIKE SUCCESS

They find the more they taste success...the more they hunger for it.

WINNERS KNOW ACCESS TO SUCCESS IS THROUGH THE MIND

They know if their mind can believe
it...they can achieve it.

WINNERS SEE POSSIBILITIES IN IMPOSSIBILITIES

They see the possibility of success...
where no one has succeeded before.

Nick Baker, 1992 Olympic Coach and Founder of Peak Performance Swim Camp, shares his recipe for winning in his book, *101 Winning Ways*. Coach Baker believes that given the right attitudes any swimmer can be a winner. *101 Winning Ways* delivers these attitudes one inspiring page at a time.

Here's An Idea . . .
Keep a copy of *101 Winning Ways* by your bedside and read a page a night, just before you go off to sleep. Consider the meaning behind the words and imagine yourself with that winning way. How would it change your swimming? How would it change your life?

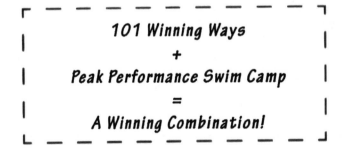

101 Winning Ways
+
Peak Performance Swim Camp
=
A Winning Combination!

www.swimcamp.com

Made in the USA
Middletown, DE
21 July 2015